J 550 Twi
Twist, Clint
Extreme Earth

$19.95
ocn664842415
10/05/2011

Ripley's EXTREME EARTH

Believe It or Not!®

PUBLISHERS

Mason Crest Publishers

TWISTS

Written by Clint Twist, Lisa Regan,
Camilla de la Bedoyere

Consultant Barbara Taylor

Originally published by

Ripley
PUBLISHING

Publisher Anne Marshall

Managing Editor Rebecca Miles
Picture Researcher James Proud
Editors Lisa Regan, Rosie Alexander
Assistant Editor Amy Harrison
Proofreader Judy Barratt
Indexer Hilary Bird

Art Director Sam South
Design Rocket Design (East Anglia) Ltd
Reprographics Stephan Davis

www.masoncrest.com

ISBN 978-1-4222-1829-7 (hardcover)

ISBN 978-1-4222-2067-2 (ppk)

Series ISBN (8 titles): 978-1-4222-1827-3

10 9 8 7 6 5 4 3 2 1

For information regarding permission, write to VP Intellectual Property, Ripley Entertainment Inc., Suite 188, 7576 Kingspointe Parkway, Orlando, Florida 32819

e-mail: publishing@ripleys.com

Library of Congress Cataloging-in-Publication Data is available.

Printed in USA

PUBLISHER'S NOTE

While every effort has been made to verify the accuracy of the entries in this book, the Publishers cannot be held responsible for any errors contained in the work. They would be glad to receive any information from readers.

WARNING

Some of the stunts and activities in this book are undertaken by experts and should not be attempted by anyone without adequate training and supervision.

CONTENTS

PAGE 23

TWISTS

WHAT OUR HOME ON EARTH!

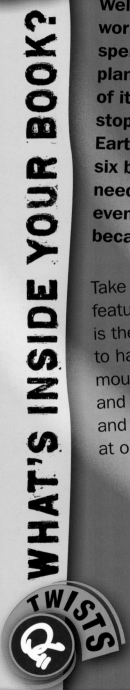

WHAT'S INSIDE YOUR BOOK?

Welcome to your world! It's easy to spend your time on this planet, making the most of its rich resources, without stopping to think about what the Earth is really like. It's home to over six billion people, and provides all we need: food, water, shelter, energy, and even the air that we breathe is safe because of Earth's atmosphere.

Take a look around and you'll see amazing features of breathtaking beauty. Earth is the only planet in our Solar System to have our spectacular combination of mountains, oceans, volcanoes, deserts, and rainforests. So read on and prepare to be amazed at our world.

Do the twist

This book is packed with superb sights created by nature. It will teach you amazing things about our planet, but like all Twists books, it shines a spotlight on things that are unbelievable but true. Turn the pages and find out more...

Learn fab fast facts to go with the cool pictures.

HOT AND COLD

These Japanese macaques like it hot—even when it's cold. They keep warm in winter temperatures of 5°F by bathing in natural hot springs. Macaque babies also roll snowballs, just for fun!

TWISTS

EARTH EXTREMES...

Coldest	Hottest	Windiest	Wettest (average)
Antarctica −129°F	El Azizia, Ethiopia 136°F	Antarctica 190 mph	Mount Wai-'ale-'ale, Kauai, Hawaii, about 500 inches a year

Found a new word? Big word alerts will explain it for you.

Ripley explains some of the geographical know-how behind features on our planet.

Don't forget to look out for the "twist it!" column on some pages. Twist the book to find out more fast facts about the world we live in.

ROOF of the WORLD
MIGHTY MOUNTAINS

...ajestic mountain ranges are nature's ...ay of showing off! Their spectacular ...eaks are capped in clouds and mist ...and cloaked with snow and ice.

Mountains are created by the slow-moving forces that cause the Earth's plates to collide. Over time, rock is thrust upward, crumpling and folding into beautiful shapes. It takes millions of years, but as soon as mountains form, erosion and weathering start to wear them down. As ice freezes and thaws near the peaks, rocks split and break away, leaving sharp pyramid-like tops, while running water and glaciers produce softer, more rounded edges. Eventually, the mountains will be completely worn away!

BIG WORD ALERT!
SUMMIT A summit is the highest part of a mountain.

Ripley explains...

Mountains are pushed upward!

Continental crust   Continental crust

Plates move together

When two continental plates collide, the rocks on both plates become compressed (squashed) and folded. Over millions of years, the folds are forced higher and higher above the surrounding surface. Mountains are formed in this way.

twist it!

...nts, and an overcoat."

A US expedition to the Himalayas in the 1960s was followed by a pilgrim from Nepal, who trekked barefoot through the snow and slept outdoors in temperatures as low as −20°F wearing just a shirt.

Mona Mule Parl and Pem Dorjee Sherpa were the first couple to get married at the top of Mount Everest, the world's highest peak. They exchanged their vows there in May 2005.

The highest mountain in the USA (outside Alaska) is Mount Whitney. California. It is less than 80 miles from Zabriskie Point in Death Valley—the lowest point in the USA.

HIGH HOPES
The Caledonian Mountains of Scotland were once part of the Appalachian Mountains in North America, until they became separated by the Atlantic Ocean as plates moved apart.

New Zealand's highest peak is Mount Cook. In 1991 the top 33 feet fell off in an avalanche.

Mount Everest is known as Sagarmatha in Nepalese.

...ld's second highest mountain ... It is nearly 800 feet ... Everest.

The tallest peaks are in the Himalayas in southern Asia. The world's highest mountain, Mount Everest in Nepal, is here and measures 29,035 feet. The Himalayas were formed when the Indian and Eurasian plates collided about 45 million years ago.

...s are a collection of the ...n each continent. The ... all seven was Canadian

...nali (20,320 feet)
...oncagua (22,830 feet)
...,510 feet)
...(19,340 feet)
...35 feet)
...nz Pyramid (16,023 feet)
...assif (16,067 feet)

There are two "base camps" on Everest, both at just over 17,000 feet. Climbers camp there on the way up and down the mountain, eating, resting, and acclimatizing (getting used to being so high up).

ICED DINNER
Seven people sat down to eat a five-course meal that they had prepared on a mountain in Tibet. They carried their food, plus table, chairs, silver cutlery, wine, flowers, and candles to a height of 22,000 feet, and even dressed the part with top hats and smart suits and ties.

Mountain memorial
A giant face in the rocky mountainside in South Dakota's Black Hills forms part of a memorial to the area's Native Americans. The sculpture was started in 1948 and still has lots of work to be done—eventually the whole mountain will have a whole figure riding a horse. It is being blasted out of the rock to honor Ohler Crazy Horse.

FASCINATING FACT

563 FEET HIGH!

13

RARE ROCK
A stone covered with long white "hair" is so rare it has been valued at over a million dollars. The hair is strands of fossilized fungus formed over millions of years.

Twists are all about Believe It or Not: amazing facts, feats, and things that will make you go "Wow!".

Look for the Ripley R to find out even more than you knew before!

Driest
Atacama Desert, Chile, no rain since records began

Tallest
Mount Everest 29,035 feet

Deepest
Pacific Ocean (Mariana Trench) 35,837 feet

Iciest
Antarctica has 90 percent of Earth's ice

OUR PLACE IN SPACE

Welcome to planet Earth, a spinning ball of hot rock that flies through space at more than 67,000 miles an hour. The world is our home and we love it! Earth is one of eight planets that circles the Sun, and the Sun is just one of billions of stars in our galaxy—the Milky Way. What makes Earth so special? So far, it's the only place in the entire Universe we know of where life exists.

Feeling dizzy? You should be, because you're not only flying around the Sun, you're also spinning at 1,000 miles an hour as the Earth turns. It's the way the Earth spins on its own axis, and orbits the Sun, that gives us measurements of time, including our 24-hour days, our 365-day years and our seasons.

SUN

It takes eight minutes for light from the Sun to reach the Earth. It is the Sun's light and heat, and the fact that Earth has water and a safe atmosphere, that allows life on Earth.

YOU ARE HERE

Earth facts

- Diameter: 7,928 miles
- Circumference: 25,000 miles
- Surface area: 200 million square miles
- Estimated mass: 5,976 billion billion tons
- Distance from Sun: 93 million miles

Ripley's Believe It or Not!®

OLD MAN

Human ancestors have been on Earth for millions of years. Scientists think that people similar to us developed around 250,000 years ago. This 5,000-year-old ice-preserved body helps scientists learn about people from the past.

Loving life

Living things are grouped into five kingdoms. The smallest unit in these kingdoms is the species, which consists of all the organisms that share the same characteristics. All species have a Latin name. The name of our own species is *Homo sapiens* (which means "wise man"). Which kingdom do you think we fit into?

ANIMALS
- Can move around
- Cannot make their own food
- Have more than one cell

PLANTS
- Are usually green
- Can make their own food
- Have more than one cell

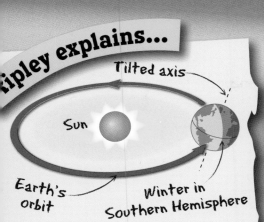

Tilted axis

Sun

Earth's orbit

Winter in Southern Hemisphere

The Earth is tilted in relation to the Sun. As the Earth makes its 365-day journey around the Sun, different parts of it are tilted toward, or away from, the Sun's light and heat. The Sun's light and heat hit the different places on Earth at different angles, giving some places more sunlight in summer and less in winter.

SUPER PLANET

The largest animal species that has ever lived is alive today. A full-grown blue whale can reach 100 feet in length and weigh 150 tons.

Scientists estimate there are about 20 million different living species on Earth, of which only about 10 percent have been identified and described.

A mushroom fossil found in Myanmar, Asia, is thought to be as much as 100 million years old.

The Earth is slowing down! It is spinning on its axis less quickly, and scientists say it may be significant enough for days in the future to have 25 hours instead of 24.

Fossils of sea creatures have been found near the top of Mount Everest.

twist it!

BIG WORD ALERT

AXIS
Imaginary line drawn through the center of the Earth from the North Pole to the South Pole.

Fossil finds

Fossils are living things that have been turned to rock over millions of years. They provide evidence of creatures that lived long ago, and allow scientists to work out what has been happening with life on our planet.

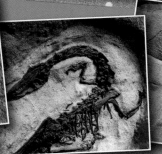

FUNGI

- Cannot make their own food
- Produce spores, not seeds e.g. yeast, mould
- Have more than one cell

PROTISTA

- Have only one cell
- Often live in soil or water e.g. amoeba

MONERA

- Have only one cell
- Very simple e.g. bacteria

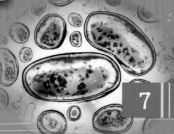

CRACKING UP
A LOOK INSIDE

There are 14 large plates and 38 smaller plates. Seven of the larger plates roughly match up to the continents of the world.

The plates carrying North America and Europe are moving away from one another at a speed of about 6 feet every 75 years. That means the two continents are getting farther away from each other at about the same rate your fingernails are growing!

The world is cracking up! The planet's outermost layer is a thick band of rock, called the crust—and it's in pieces. These pieces, known as plates, fit together like a giant jigsaw puzzle.

Strangely, plates are always on the move, stretching and squashing into one another as their edges grow or get sucked down into a super-hot layer of molten rock below. This whole fantastical process is called plate tectonics, and these crusty clashes are to blame for volcanoes, rift valleys, mountains, and earthquakes.

About 250 million years ago, all of today's landmasses were joined in one super-continent called Pangaea. As the Earth's plates moved, at maximum speeds of just 4¾ inches a year, it was pulled apart.

Mantle

Crust

Inner core

Outer core

The Earth has three layers: the crust, the mantle, and the core. The mantle is a thick layer of molten (liquid) rock with temperatures up to 5,800°F. Below is Earth's core where temperatures rise above 9,000°F. The outer core is liquid, but the pressure keeps the inner core solid.

The supercontinent of Pangaea was surrounded by a single ocean called Panthalassa. Look carefully at this map and you might see some familiar continent shapes.

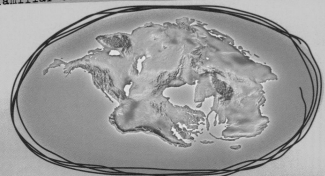

Hot stuff

It's your fault

Some of the world's worst earthquakes happen along fault lines. The San Andreas Fault in California marks the boundary between the Pacific and North American plates. The fault line extends at least 10 miles into the Earth, and stretches for over 700 miles from north to south.

AROUND THE WORLD

The interior of the Earth is kept hot by heat from when the planet first formed, heat produced by radioactive elements, and heat from small dense particles colliding as they sink toward the center of the Earth.

Although the Earth's crust is made of rock and is solid, it is actually nearly 50 percent oxygen.

The South Pacific island of Niuatoputapu is the fastest-moving place on Earth, moving at 10 inches a year.

Margaret Hegarty of Concord, North Carolina, is the oldest woman to run a marathon on each of the seven continents. She was 76 when she completed the task, but has carried on running well into her 80s.

twist it!

Lava lover

Volcanic craters are a kind of window to the inner Earth. The hot, molten rock (called magma) in the mantle can push its way to the surface, where it comes out as lava.

Patrick Koster from the Netherlands has spent ten years photographing volcanoes and loves them so much that he proposed to his wife at the edge of a crater. He even reorganized his honeymoon so that he didn't miss a major eruption.

SHOCKS AND SHAKES

EARTH'S POWER

Hold on tight—the Earth's moving! For a few terrifying seconds the ground shakes and quakes. Buildings topple and great cracks appear in the Earth's surface as it rips open—this is the awesome power of an earthquake.

These mighty Earth movements happen in an instant, but they build up over a long time. As the Earth's plates grind against one another they build up tension. One sudden slip is all it takes for all that stored energy to be released, with ferocious force. Entire cities may be destroyed in an earthquake, bringing misery, chaos, and death.

Japan has many Earth tremors every year. Most of them are too small to cause much damage. However, in 1995, a massive earthquake hit the area around the city of Kobe. Nearly 7,000 people died and over 45,000 homes were ruined. The raised section of the Hanshin motorway collapsed during the quake, which only lasted for about 20 seconds.

The epicenter of the Kobe quake was miles below the Earth's surface.

It cost over $1 billion to repair and rebuild the city.

Many "aftershocks" caused more damage after the main quake.

Read all about it

The exact location of an earthquake is known as the epicenter. Scientists use sensitive instruments known as seismographs to measure the energy waves from an earthquake. By combining readings from seismographs around the world, they can work out the position of the epicenter.

DISASTER STRIKES SAN FRANCISCO

An earthquake lasting only a minute struck San Francisco at 5:12 this morning, and has caused the worst damage seen in this nation's history. Fires are raging through the city, leaving people without homes, work, belongings, and loved ones.

Eyewitnesses report seeing buildings crushed like a cracker in your hand, the ground moving in waves like the ocean, and the earth slipping from beneath their feet. Some streets have sunk by 4 feet; others have been pushed up to form 5-foot-high waves of rubble.

QUAKE UPDATE:

April 30, 1906

The fires in San Francisco burned for three days. Over a quarter of a million people were made homeless, and at least 3,000 people were killed. Nearly 500 city blocks—at least 25,000 buildings—were destroyed.

ALL SHOOK UP

The island of Ranongga in the South Pacific was lifted out of the water by 10 feet in 2007, by an earthquake that measured 8.1 on the Richter scale.

An earthquake in Mexico in 1985 was strong enough to shake water out of a swimming pool 1,240 miles away in Tucson, Arizona.

Hundreds of hibernating snakes came out from their underground hideaways in China, just before an earthquake struck in 1975.

A 2007 earthquake was powerful enough to throw back a torpedo boat that had sunk in World War II.

The shock waves forming an earthquake can travel between 3¾ miles a second and 6¾ miles a second, depending whether they are in the Earth's core or near the surface.

Clever creatures

Japanese scientists believe the deep-sea oarfish, which usually lives at depths of more than 650 feet, helps them to predict earthquakes by appearing at the surface before tremors are felt.

One result of earthquakes is that the shaking can cause some soils to behave like liquids, so that buildings sink into the ground.

>>Double disaster<<

The mountainous province of Sichuan in southwest China was hit by an earthquake in May, 2008. Nearly 90,000 people were either killed or reported missing. A year later, a landslide destroyed this bridge—part of a main road used while trying to rebuild the devastated area—killing even more people.

twist it!

ROOF of the WORLD
MIGHTY MOUNTAINS

Majestic mountain ranges are nature's way of showing off! Their spectacular peaks are capped in clouds and mist and cloaked with snow and ice.

Mountains are created by the slow-moving forces that cause the Earth's plates to collide. Over time, rock is thrust upward, crumpling and folding into beautiful shapes. It takes millions of years, but as soon as mountains form, erosion and weathering start to wear them down. As ice freezes and thaws near the peaks, rocks split and break away, leaving sharp pyramid-like tops, while running water and glaciers produce softer, more rounded edges. Eventually, the mountains will be completely worn away!

New Zealand's highest peak is Mount Cook. In 1991 the top 33 feet fell off in an avalanche.

Mount Everest is known as Sagarmatha in Nepalese.

K2 is the world's second highest mountain. It is nearly 800 feet shorter than Everest.

The tallest peaks are in the Himalayas in southern Asia. The world's highest mountain, Mount Everest in Nepal, is here and measures 29,035 feet. The Himalayas were formed when the Indian and Eurasian plates collided about 45 million years ago.

The Seven Summits are a collection of the highest mountains on each continent. The first person to climb all seven was Canadian Pat Morrow in 1986.

- North America: Denali (20,320 feet)
- South America: Aconcagua (22,830 feet)
- Europe: Elbrus (18,510 feet)
- Africa: Kilimanjaro (19,340 feet)
- Asia: Everest (29,035 feet)
- Australasia: Carstenz Pyramid (16,023 feet)
- Antarctic: Vinson Massif (16,067 feet)

There are two "base camps" on Everest, both at just over 17,000 feet. Climbers camp there on the way up and down the mountain, eating, resting, and acclimatizing (getting used to being so high up).

BIG WORD ALERT

SUMMIT
A summit is the highest part of a mountain.

Ripley explains...

Mountains are pushed upward

Continental crust

Continental crust

Plates move together

When two continental plates collide, the rocks on both plates become compressed (squashed) and folded. Over millions of years, the folds are forced higher and higher above the surrounding surface. Mountains are formed in this way.

HIGH HOPES

The Caledonian Mountains of Scotland were once part of the Appalachian Mountains in North America, until they became separated by the Atlantic Ocean as plates moved apart.

The highest mountain in the USA (outside Alaska) is Mount Whitney, California. It is less than 80 miles from Zabriskie Point in Death Valley—the lowest point in the USA.

Mona Mule Pati and Pem Dorjee Sherpa were the first couple to get married at the top of Mount Everest, the world's highest peak. They exchanged their vows there in May 2005.

A US expedition to the Himalayas in the 1960s was followed by a pilgrim from Nepal, who trekked barefoot through the snow and slept outdoors in temperatures as low as −20°F wearing just a shirt, pants, and an overcoat.

ICED DINNER

Seven people sat down to eat a five-course meal that they had prepared on a mountain in Tibet. They carried their food, plus table, chairs, silver cutlery, wine, flowers, and candles to a height of 22,000 feet, and even dressed the part with top hats and smart suits and ties.

Mountain memorial

A giant face in the rocky mountainside in South Dakota's Black Hills forms part of a memorial to the area's Native Americans. The sculpture was started in 1948 and still has lots of work to be done—eventually the mountain will have a whole figure riding a horse. It is being blasted out of the rock to honor Chief Crazy Horse.

FASCINATING FACT!

563 FEET HIGH!

VIOLENT ERUPTIONS
VOLCANOES

When a mountain comes to life, and starts spouting smoke and spewing lava, it's clearly no ordinary mountain. Mighty volcanoes sit on top of the Earth's hot spots.

Super-heated rock bubbles quietly beneath the surface until its energy can no longer be contained—and an explosive force erupts. Boiling liquid rock, poisonous gases, ash, and volcanic bombs all spew out of active volcanoes, spelling tragedy and devastation for people living nearby. When volcanoes are quiet, between eruptions, they are described as dormant, and when they are no longer active at all, volcanoes are said to be extinct.

The temperature of lava inside a crater can reach 2,700°F, that's nearly one third the temperature of the Sun's surface.

The 1883 eruption of Krakatoa created a tsunami that was 130 feet high.

The Indonesian volcano Krakatoa killed over 36,000 people when it erupted in 1883. 165 towns and villages were destroyed and another 132 were badly damaged. Debris was blown 22 miles into the sky, and the noise of the eruption could be heard over 4,500 miles away in Sri Lanka. In 2009, the volcano began erupting again.

Bubbling unde

The mud-filled crater of Totumo volcano in Colombia is a popular bathing spot! The hot mud is supposed to have beneficial effects on the human body.

Twist it!

The world's tallest volcano is Ojos del Salado in the South American Andes. It towers 22,608 feet above sea level, on the Chile–Argentina border.

Volcanic stones, known as pumice stones, are full of trapped air so weigh much less than you would expect. It's possible to lift a pumice stone twice your own size.

The volcano rabbit is found only on the slopes of four volcanoes near Mexico City, Mexico.

Some 60 percent of the population of Central America lives within 25 miles of an active or dormant volcano.

The world's largest volcano is Mauna Loa (height 13,681 feet), which occupies about half the island of Hawaii.

READY STEADY BLOW!

IN HOT WATER

Extreme surfer CJ Kanuha surfed within 20 feet of the lava flow from Kilauea volcano on Hawaii's Big Island. The molten rock heats the sea to 400°F and it melted the wax on his surfboard.

Ripley explains...

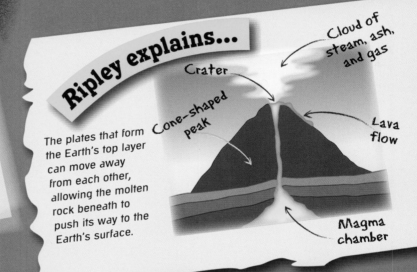

The plates that form the Earth's top layer can move away from each other, allowing the molten rock beneath to push its way to the Earth's surface.

Cloud of steam, ash, and gas

Crater

Cone-shaped peak

Lava flow

Magma chamber

Buried in ash

79 AD Mount Vesuvius erupted and buried the Roman town of Pompeii under 20 feet ash. Archeologists discovered casts of the bodies of some of the unfortunate inhabitants who were buried as they tried to hide or escape.

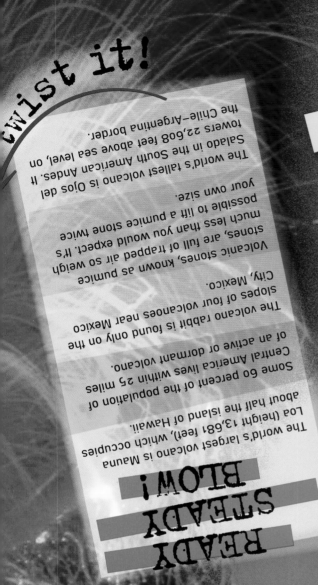

Blown sky high

This photograph is of Sarychev Peak, next door to Russia and Japan. It erupted in 2009, blowing a 5-mile tower of smoke, ash, and steam into the air and through a hole blown in the clouds by the force. The picture was taken from the International Space Station, orbiting the Earth.

BIG WORD ALERT

MAGMA
The molten rock from deep inside the Earth. It is called lava once it has made its way to the surface.

REAL HARD

ROCKS AND MINERALS

Think rocks are dull? Think again, because some of them are shiny or colorful, and a few even contain precious minerals and gems, such as diamonds! There are three main types of rock: igneous, metamorphic, and sedimentary.

The type of rock that forms in the Earth's crust depends on three things: temperature, pressure, and the recipe of minerals it contains. When these three factors play their part, a soup of minerals can be transformed into different rocks, such as a smooth, sparkling white marble, or a salt-and-pepper patterned granite. And if rocks get very hot and squashed again, they melt back into a mineral magma soup!

FIRE ROCKS

Igneous rocks form from magma that has cooled and turned hard when it came close to, or burst through, the Earth's surface. The Giant's Causeway on the coast of Northern Ireland is made up of about 40,000 columns of the igneous rock basalt that were pushed up millions of years ago.

Igneous rocks are sometimes called fire rocks because they were formed from volcanic material.

SET IN STONE

Sedimentary rocks are formed from sediments, such as sand and clay, that are deposited by wind and water. These amazing sandstone stripes are part of the Coyote Buttes and are known as The Wave. They were formed around 190 million years ago on the border of Arizona and Utah, USA. Over time, the sandstone has been eroded into the fascinating swirling shapes.

Rock formation

These may look just like piles of stones—very cleverly balanced, you must admit—but they're more than that. They are "inukshuk," stone landmarks built by many Arctic people. Enukso Point on Baffin Island, Canada, is a national historic site containing over 100 of these stone structures.

ROCK 'N' ROLL

Certain types of the sedimentary rock limestone are composed entirely of the compressed shells of prehistoric sea creatures.

In 1906, a miner named Lindsay Hicks was buried inside Granite Mountain, California, after a mine cave-in. He was covered by thousands of tons of rock, but was rescued unharmed after 15 days.

Rocks have been forming and changing for millions of years. If you climb the Guadalupe Mountains in Texas you will be touching limestone that was once a tropical reef, about 250 million years ago.

twist it!

BIG WORD ALERT

GEOLOGISTS
Scientists who study rocks.

Ripley's Believe It or Not!®

RARE ROCK

A stone covered with long white "hair" is so rare it has been valued at over a million dollars. The hair is strands of fossilized fungus formed over millions of years.

ALL CHANGE

Metamorphic rocks are rocks that have been metamorphosed (changed into something else) by volcanic heat and pressure. Slate, for example, is metamorphosed shale, and limestone turns into marble. Many of the world's mountain ranges contain metamorphic rocks. These rocks in the Swiss Alps have been changed further by glacier movement smoothing and scratching them.

GOING UNDERGROUND

CAVES AND MINES

Hidden from view, below the ground, are some of the Earth's most amazing natural wonders. Enormous caves and labyrinths of tunnels weave between solid rocks, carved out by the powerful force of water.

Rainwater and river water can seep through the cracks in rocks to form underground rivers. Water also dissolves some rocks, such as limestone, turning it into a liquid that drips and hardens again, to create amazing stalactites and stalagmites.

Some tunnels and caves owe more to people power. Valuable minerals such as coal form deep underground, and miners remove them by cutting into the rock, creating tunnels and caves.

The crystals are made of gypsum and are translucent.

The biggest crystals are 39 feet long.

CRYSTAL CAVE

These crystal daggers are as long as a bus! They were found by miners in 2000, around a thousand feet below the ground. They are part of the Naica Mine in Mexico, which has other caves containing smaller—but still spectacular—crystal formations.

Miners had to pump water out of the cave to clear it.

Light up, light up

Cave tours in New Zealand let you see in the dark! The roof of this cave is covered with glowing fireflies. The creatures are actually beetles and can flash their lights to attract other fireflies. They make the light on their abdomen by allowing air to mix with a special substance they produce.

The world's longest system of underground caves is the Mammoth Cave complex below Kentucky, USA, which extends over 352 miles—about the distance from Los Angeles to San Francisco—and has a maximum depth of 377 feet.

Temperatures in Coober Pedy, in the Australian outback, reach an uncomfortable 120°F, and so the people there have moved somewhere cooler: underground. There are a range of houses to choose from, plus museums, shops, churches, and hotels.

COOL DOWN

DEEP THOUGHTS

The deepest oil well ever drilled is the Tiber well that goes is 35,055 feet below the seabed in the Gulf of Mexico. This means that the bottom of the well is more than 39,000 feet below sea level, and deeper than Mount Everest is high.

Blackwater rafting is a thrill-a-minute sport that takes participants through the caves of New Zealand—on an inner tube! Underground rivers carry along the tubes through dark passages that can be full of eels.

Starting in 1906, William Schmidt spent 38 years digging an underground passage through the El Paso Mountains of California. He burrowed for 2,087 feet and through 2,600 tons of rock.

twist it!

BIG WORD ALERT

SPELEOLOGY
The science of exploring underground spaces.

19

COMFORT BLANKET

THE ATMOSPHERE

The atmosphere around our planet keeps it nice and cosy! This thick layer of air is a rich mix of gases that protects us from the burning rays of the Sun, and keeps the heat in at night, like a comforting blanket.

That's not all we have to thank the atmosphere for: one of its top jobs is creating climate. The bottom layer of the atmosphere is called the troposphere and this is where weather happens. Liquid water spends part of its time as water vapor, high in the sky, and some of the water that falls today as rain was once drunk by dinosaurs!

The auroras are sometimes called the Northern Lights or Southern Lights.

SKY LIGHTS

Amazing light displays appear in the highest layers of the atmosphere and can be seen near the North and South poles. They are called the aurora borealis (say or-ora bor-ee-ar-lis) in the north and aurora australis (say or-ora os-trar-lis) in the south. The lights are created by a reaction between atoms from the Sun and gases in the Earth's atmosphere.

Sometimes the lights move and dance or shimmer.

Ripley's Believe It or Not!®

All ha

Hailstones can grow really big—these ones found after a hailstorm in Kansas in 1999.

HEAD IN THE CLOUDS

Clouds form different shapes at different heights, and depending how much water or ice they contain. Thin, wispy clouds high in the sky are known as cirrus clouds. This one, seen over Wellington in New Zealand, has been blown into the shape of a deer!

ipley explains...

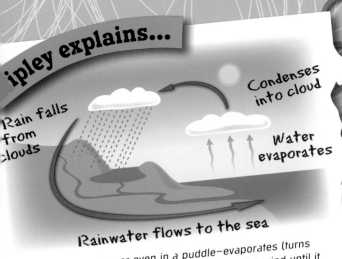

Rain falls from clouds

Condenses into cloud

Water evaporates

Rainwater flows to the sea

Water in the oceans—or even in a puddle—evaporates (turns to gas) and mixes with the air. It is carried by the wind until it condenses (turns back to water), making clouds. It falls back to the ground as precipitation and the cycle starts all over again.

>> Blown away <<

This house was damaged by a tornado—it had one end blown off completely, but the inside was left intact. The dishes in the pantry weren't even broken!

FASCINATING FACT! FASCINATING FACT! FASCINATING FACT!

Twist it!

Up to 100 tons of space dust falls into the Earth's atmosphere every day. That's about the same weight as 20 African elephants.

NASA satellites have shown that the two sunniest places in the world are patches in the Pacific Ocean, south of Hawaii, and in the Sahara Desert in Niger.

Mount Waialeale, on Kauai in Hawaii, has rain nearly every day of the year. Only a few miles away on the coast, they get as little rain as 20 inches in a whole year.

Within the troposphere, the air temperature drops by about 3.6°F per 1,000 feet of altitude.

RAIN OR SHINE

BIG WORD ALERT

PRECIPITATION
Any kind of wetness coming from the sky: rain, snow, sleet, hail, and even fog.

FUNNEL VISION

A tornado is a whirling funnel of air formed in some thunderstorms. They can travel at high speeds of 250 mph and cause chaos and destruction. They happen in many parts of the world, but are frequent and famous in the central states of the USA, which are known as "tornado alley."

BEND IT

A rainbow is formed by sunlight being refracted (bent) by raindrops. You will only see a rainbow if the sun is behind you.

UP IN THE AIR

WILD WEATHER

Take a look outside—is the weather looking wild or mild? Right this moment there are about 2,000 thunderstorms and 100 flashes of lightning zapping through the sky, all over the world. Just one flash of supercharged lightning contains enough energy to light 150 million light bulbs!

Extreme weather might get you off school, but it can play havoc with people's lives. In the globe's cold spots, temperatures dip below a supercool 5°F in winter, while coastal areas can be hit by storm surges, gale force winds, and heavy rains that bring cliffs crashing to the ground.

- An average lightning storm can discharge sufficient power to supply the entire USA with electricity for 20 minutes.

- In 1998, during a soccer game in the Democratic Republic of Congo, all 11 players on one team were killed by lightning. None of the other team was struck.

- A single lightning strike in Utah, in 1918, killed 504 sheep in one blast.

- Ray Cauldwell, a baseball pitcher for the Cleveland Indians, was struck by lightning while playing. He was knocked unconscious but came to and carried on playing—and was on the winning side!

Kenneth Libbrecht of California has found a way to take photos of snowflakes. The results are beautiful, and show the six-sided formation of each individual flake.

CRYSTAL CLEAR

If the air in the atmosphere is cold enough, the rising water vapor (see Ripley explains, page 21) freezes instead of turning to liquid. This forms six-sided crystals: snowflakes. The air near the ground needs to be below freezing, too, or the crystals will turn to rain as they fall.

FREAKY FREEZE

Residents near Lake Geneva were shocked by scenes in January 2005. Gale-force winds carried water droplets from the lake, which froze on anything in their path because of 10°F temperatures.

Really wild

A hurricane is the most awesomely powerful of all weather events. The largest hurricanes extend 600–1,000 miles in diameter and produce winds up to 200 mph. They are caused by rising warm air over the ocean. As the storm reaches land, it begins to die out— but can still last for days and cause devastating damage.

SNOW DONUTS

These amazing snow rollers, or snow donuts, are formed naturally when a clump of soft snow falls into hard snow at the top of a slope. They are quite rare, but Mike Stanford found these ones in Washington State in 2007 that were big enough to poke his head through!

HOME ALONE

A hurricane raged across Texas in 2008 and completely flattened buildings and trees. The only house left standing in one area was that of Warren and Pam Adams. They had lost a previous home to a 2005 hurricane, so had wisely built their new one on 14-foot-high columns to withstand the storms.

>> Fenced in <<

The 2008 hurricane in Texas left these fish high and dry! The storms caused huge floods, which carried these fish up to 4 feet high and left them stuck in the links of a fence.

WATERWORLD

OCEAN COMMOTION

We call our planet Earth, but a better name might be Water—because more than 70 percent of the world's surface is actually covered by oceans and seas.

The biggest and deepest ocean is the Pacific and it contains more than half of the entire planet's seawater.

While lakes and rivers have fresh water, which we can drink, oceans and seas are salty. There are five main zones, or layers, in the oceans, from just below the surface to the darkest depths.

0-656 feet

656-3,280 feet

The menacing-looking fangtooth fish only grows to about 6 inches, but its teeth are the largest of any ocean fish compared to its body size.

The maximum depth humans can reach with scuba equipment is just less than 1,000 feet.

SUNLIGHT (EPIPELAGIC) ZONE

The ferocious bull shark swims close to humans shore, so is a potential danger to humans taking a swim. They live in the warm waters of the ocean, but can also swim upriver and don't mind the fresh waters of the Amazon and Mississippi.

Jellyfish are found in all of the world's oceans. They have no heart, brain, or blood and use their tentacles to trap food.

Free divers such as Herbert Nitsch from Austria, can dive to 700 feet with no breathing equipment except their lungs.

TWILIGHT (MESOPELAGIC) ZONE

twist it!

In 1990 ocean adventurer Tom McClean sailed across the Atlantic in a boat shaped like a bottle. Onboard he had a four poster bed!

From the top of Mount Irazu in Costa Rica you can see both the Pacific Ocean and the Atlantic Ocean.

Columbus landed in America in the 15th century.

The Atlantic Ocean is still growing at a rate of 1½ inches per year. This means it was about 66 feet narrower when Columbus landed in America in the 15th century.

Scientists have calculated that there are about the same number of molecules in a spoonful of water as there are spoonfuls of water in the Atlantic Ocean.

MAKING A SPLASH

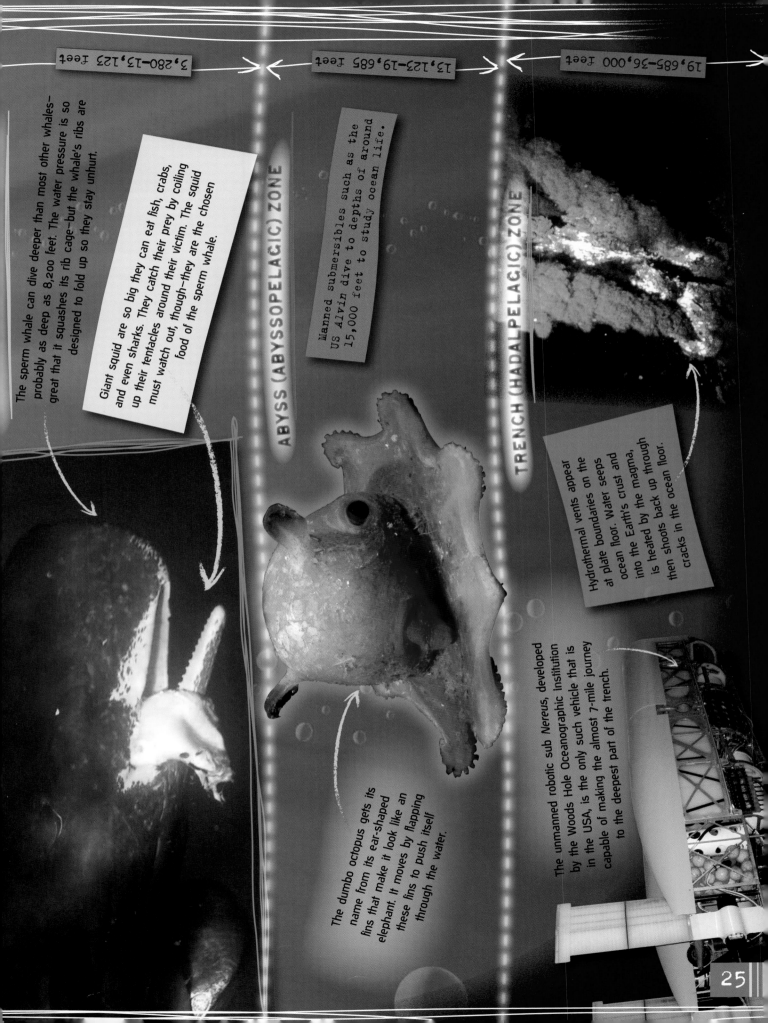

The sperm whale can dive deeper than most other whales—probably as deep as 8,200 feet. The water pressure is so great that it squashes its rib cage—but the whale's ribs are designed to fold up so they stay unhurt.

Giant squid are so big they can eat fish, crabs, and even sharks. They catch their prey by coiling up their tentacles around their victim. The squid must watch out, though—they are the chosen food of the sperm whale.

Manned submersibles such as the US Alvin dive to depths of around 15,000 feet to study ocean life.

ABYSS (ABYSSOPELAGIC) ZONE

TRENCH (HADALPELAGIC) ZONE

Hydrothermal vents appear at plate boundaries on the ocean floor. Water seeps into the Earth's crust and is heated by the magma, then shoots back up through cracks in the ocean floor.

The dumbo octopus gets its name from its ear-shaped fins that make it look like an elephant. It moves by flapping these fins to push itself through the water.

The unmanned robotic sub Nereus, developed by the Woods Hole Oceanographic Institution in the USA, is the only such vehicle that is capable of making the almost 7-mile journey to the deepest part of the trench.

REMARKABLE REEFS
CORAL AND THE TROPICS

Coral reefs can grow enormous, but they are built by tiny animals that are no bigger than your fingernail!

Reefs are rocky structures that are home to little squashy polyps, which are related to sea anemones and jellyfish. The polyps use minerals from the water to create rocky cups around themselves. Over many years, thousands of polyps add to a reef, and it grows bigger. Lots of other animals find refuge in the reef and become part of a precious ecosystem. Polyps grow best in warm, shallow, and clean water in the tropics just north and south of the Equator.

Many of the species living in reefs look like plants, but are animals that feed on fish and animal scraps.

400 species of coral make up the Great Barrier Reef.

Around 1,500 species of fish live on the Great Barrier Reef.

The world's largest reef is the Great Barrier Reef, which runs some 1,250 miles along the eastern coast of Australia and covers an area of about 80,000 square miles.

Reef-building corals need sunlight and cannot live below about 200 feet. They are also very sensitive to water temperature and cannot tolerate changes of more than about 1.8°F. Coral polyps can be as small as 0.1 inches, but they form colonies up to 60 inches across.

Hideaways

Many reef-dwellers use camouflage to keep them safe in the sea. They may choose bright colors and hide in the coral itself, or disguise themselves with sandy colors to burrow into the seabed.

COMMON OCTOPUS

Ripley's Believe It or Not!®

Toothy monsters

Moray eels cannot swallow their prey. Instead, they have a second set of teeth in their throat, which move forward to grab the prey and pull it into their body to digest.

DIVE IN!

Coral reefs are very fragile, and each year boat propellers, anchors, fishing nets, and careless divers damage large areas of reef.

Beware of the attractive red fire coral—if touched with bare skin the coral polyps will deliver a nasty sting.

Coral reefs sometimes form ring-shaped islands, known as atolls, around the craters of undersea volcanoes.

The shallow waters off Palm Beach, Florida, are home to an unusual reef: an artificial commemorative reef, made from concrete cases containing the cremated remains of dead people.

The Great Barrier Reef is longer than the west coast of the USA.

twist it!

Cleaning up

Certain small fish have an important job on the reef—cleaning up. Larger fish allow them to swim into their mouth, without eating them, to nibble at the parasites that pester them. Some turtles visit special "cleaning stations" to get rid of unwanted hitchhikers on their shells and soft undersides.

ON THE EDGE
COASTLINES

Coasts are the world's most popular places to live, but they are also among the most dangerous. Crashing waves, storm surges, collapsing cliffs, and terrible tsunamis mark out the seashore as a place of potential peril!

The ebb and flow of tides also make their mark on coastal life and landforms. Twice a day, the water level at a shore rises and falls in a freaky phenomenon we call tides.

High tides and low tides are the result of big bulges in seawater that are caused by the Moon! As our near neighbor orbits Earth, and Earth spins, the Moon's gravity pulls on the water, forcing it to move in and out at coastlines.

Many mountaineers climb up the stack to reach the top.

The Old Man of Hoy is still being eroded and getting weaker at its base.

This tall rock is called the Old Man of Hoy. It is 449 feet high and is found in the Orkney Islands, Scotland. Rocks like this one are called sea stacks and are made when the waves crash against the coast. Eventually enough rock is worn away to leave a tower standing on its own.

The rock was probably part of the coast as little as 400 years ago.

Along steep rocky coasts, the action of the tide and waves often forms vertical cliffs. The world's tallest sea cliffs are on Canada's Baffin Island and rise some 4,500 feet above the sea.

Jim Denevan's sand art

Sand artist Jim Denevan spends up to 7 hours creating his pictures. He uses a stick washed up from the sea to draw with, and walks up to 30 miles up and down the beach. When the waves come, his work is washed away.

FIX STAMP HERE

P. Mariner
Lighthouse Road
Norfolk

Beaches are formed along gently sloping coastlines where the waves deposit sand, pebbles, and even crushed coral, which have been washed away from other parts of the coastline. Sand is made up of tiny grains of crushed and decomposed rocks, shells, and coral.

David Jones
Beach Drive
Coastville West

Jan Belcher's sand sculptures

The surface of the Earth can be eroded—worn away by wind, water (such as waves or rain), and ice.

The World islands were started in 2003. Three palm islands have also been built nearby.

Ripley's—— Believe It or Not!

This set of 300 islands has been created in the sea, 4 miles from Dubai's coast. Sand was pumped from the shallow waters and used to build new land in the shape of many of the world's countries. You can buy your own island for a minimum price of $15 million!

A WHOLE NEW WORLD

Around 11 billion cubic feet of sand have been used to make the islands.

BAY WATCH

The greatest difference between high and low tide is found in the Bay of Fundy in Canada, where the sea rises and falls as much as 56 feet twice daily.

The sand at the Hawaiian beach of Barking Sands does actually make a noise like a dog! The dry grains of sand make a strange barking sound when you walk on it barefoot.

The tallest wave to batter the coast appeared in July 1958 and hit the shores of Lituya Bay in Alaska. The wave was 1,720 feet high.

Fjords—long, narrow, and steep-sided coastal inlets—were formed when rising sea levels flooded river valleys.

Alaska's coastline is longer than the coastlines of every other US state added together.

twist it!

COOL WATERS

Water, water, everywhere! Get the umbrella out and put your boots on—more than 121,000 cubic miles of water is expected to fall on Earth in the next year. Thirsty plants will suck up most of it to make food, but about one third will flow, in streams and rivers, back to the sea. The source of a river is usually high in the mountains, and the water flows downward fast; full of energy, it carves valleys into the rock. By the time a river reaches its mouth it's worn itself out and flows more slowly, depositing sand, mud, and silt in a flood plain, as it meanders toward the sea.

Niagara Falls are the most powerful waterfalls in North America.

The falls are separated by Goat Island.

>>Fall guy<<

The first person to walk across Niagara Falls on a tightrope was Jean-François Gravelet, also known as "The Great Blondin," of France. In 1859, he used a 1,100-foot rope and walked from bank to bank, dressed in a wig, purple vest, and pantaloons. He also crossed on a bicycle, in the dark, on stilts, carrying a man on his back, with a wheelbarrow, and on one trip he carried a table and stopped in the middle to eat cake.

Take a drop

Niagara Falls, on the US-Canadian border, are unusually wide, with terrific amounts of water flowing over them. If temperatures drop low enough, an ice bridge may form across the river.

There are two waterfalls on the Niagara River: Horseshoe Falls and the American Falls.

Amazing Amazon

The world's mightiest river is the Amazon, which flows for 3,990 miles across South America. Enough fresh water pours from the Amazon into the Atlantic Ocean every day to provide the USA with the water it needs for five months–ten times the amount of water carried by the Mississippi River.

At its widest point, the Amazon is 6.8 miles wide during the dry season. During the rainy season, it grows to around 24.8 miles across. Where the Amazon opens at its estuary, the river is over 202 miles wide!

Going to great lengths

Slovenian Martin Strel has swum some of the world's greatest rivers. His most amazing achievement, in 2007, saw him swim the length of the Amazon River in only 66 days. He had to swim for up to 12 hours each day to cover the distance, in muddy waters that hide flesh-eating [f]ish, poisonous spiders, and dangerous snakes, wearing a [h]omemade mask to protect his face against sunburn.

The world's largest lake is the Caspian Sea, which borders Russia, Iran, and Turkmenistan, with a total area of about 143,000 square miles.

An incredible sight was reported at Florida's Gasparilla Lake in August 2003. Despite the lake being totally landlocked, with no links to the sea, locals saw a dolphin swimming there!

In the southwestern USA, the Colorado River has slowly cut down through solid rock to create the 277-mile-long Grand Canyon, which has an average depth of 4,060 feet.

Mountain streams in Valais, Switzerland, are home to hungry snakes, which lie in wait and grab trout that jump above the water.

The world's longest river is the Nile, which flows 4,132 miles from lake Victoria in central Africa to the Mediterranean Sea.

HIGH AND FLOW

Lakes are temporary gatherings of water that have not found their way to the sea.

Waterfalls are made where hard rock forms part of the riverbed. The flowing water cannot erode the hard rock, but does wear away the soft rock around it, forming a step in the river where the water drops over the edge.

RIVERS OF ICE

A glacier is a vast body of frozen water that flows downhill, like a river. There's one important difference though—glaciers move sooooo slooooowly that you could sit and stare at one for ages, and not spot any change.

When a glacier moves, its great weight melts the ice at its bottom, so it actually glides along on a thin film of water, like an ice skater. These rivers of ice are big and tough. Glaciers grind away at rocks creating U-shaped valleys and collecting a heavy load of rocks and pebbles. When a glacier melts, piles of pebbles might be one of the few signs that ever existed!

SLOW MOTION

Glaciers move very, very slowly. A glacier that travels a mile in a month is considered to be moving at high speed. Each snowfall adds another layer to a glacier's surface and increases the pressure on the ice beneath. The ice at the bottom of a glacier is so compressed that it looks blue.

DANGER ZONE

Cracks in a glacier, called crevasses, can be deeper than 100 feet and have steep, straight sides. Mountaineers must take care not to fall into them. That sounds easy, but sometimes a crevasse can be hidden by a snow bridge that looks safe to walk across.

True blue

This beautiful, crystal-clear pool on top of a glacier is water, not ice. The sun gets hot enough to melt the surface snow and ice and create a pool on top of the frozen layer.

SO COOL

On Greenland and Antarctica, there is so much ice, and so many glaciers, that they have joined together into vast "seas" of ice that are known as ice-sheets.

Some mountain glaciers in European ski resorts are wrapped in reflective foil to stop them from melting in summer.

A melting iceberg makes a fizzing sound, known as "Bergie Seltzer." It is caused by trapped air bubbles that pop as they are released.

An Arctic iceberg was seen at latitude 28°22′ that's just south of Daytona Beach in Florida.

There is a small glacier inside the crater of the extinct volcano Mount Kilimanjaro, located only 3 degrees south of the Equator in East Africa.

Twist it!

CALVING

Large chunks of ice may "calve" (break away) from a glacier and float out to sea as an iceberg. Some icebergs are huge: as big and heavy as two Statues of Liberty. Smaller, car-sized icebergs are known as growlers. Blue stripes may form if the ice freezes super fast and contains no air bubbles.

Wakeboarding is a mixture of surfing, snow boarding, and water skiing. Boarders are towed along on a cable and perform jumps and tricks. In July 2008, extreme wakeboarders from Florida made the trip to the Arctic to test their skills on the enormous icebergs there.

>> Berg boarding <<

FROZEN WILDERNESS

The Earth's extremes are five times colder than the inside of a freezer. These poles are places where only the strongest survive.

More than 90 percent of the world's fresh water is permanently frozen into ice at the poles. Around the North Pole there is no land, only frozen water that covers around 4 million square miles in the winter. The continent of Antarctica covers the South Pole, and has an area of 5.5 million square miles. It's almost entirely buried beneath snow and ice up to nearly 3 miles thick.

SLEEPING ON ICE

Several hotels north of the Arctic Circle make the most of the freezing conditions to attract visitors. The hotels are built from ice and snow, with beds lined with reindeer fur to keep guests cozy at night. The hotels have to be rebuilt every year.

The term Arctic is derived from the Greek arktos, meaning bear. It was named for the polar bear.

The polar bear is the world's largest land predator.

Superhuman

Lewis Gordon Pugh, a British endurance swimmer and explorer, loves the cold. In July 2007 he swam just over half a mile across the Arctic Ocean from the geographic North Pole in only 18 minutes and 50 seconds. Wearing only briefs, a cap and goggles, the temperature ranged between freezing 29°F and 32°F—brrr!

NE

N

NW

NORTH POLE

Arctic Circle

Tropic of Cancer

There are seven countries with parts inside the Arctic Circle: Russia, Finland, Sweden, Norway, Greenland, Canada, and the USA (Alaska). Most of the area known as the North Pole is frozen sea, not land.

Polar bears are found only in the Arctic region.

Wright Valley in Antarctica's McMurdo Dry Valleys is home to Lake Vanda. Parts of Lake Vanda are warm and unfrozen, but the ice that forms around the edge is said to be the clearest ice in the world.

The coldest recorded natural temperature was −128.6°F in Antarctica in July 1983.

Antarctica is the windiest place on Earth. At Commonwealth Bay, wind speed regularly reaches 200 mph.

...d is a continent, but not a country. Nobody lives there permanently. It has no cities or towns, but it does have many research stations for scientists.

SOUTH POLE

SE

SW

S

Antarctic Circle

Freezing sea

Sea ice grows in stages. Small ice needles get together as mushy grease ice. Waves and wind squash this into pancake ice. Gradually, the pancakes freeze together and become permanent pack ice. This can attach itself to land, or move around the ocean.

PANCAKE ICE

PACK ICE

FASCINATING FACT! FASCINATING FACT!

twist it!

The lowest point on Earth's land surface is the Bentley Trench in Antarctica, and it is completely covered by ice. The bottom of the trench is more than 8,000 feet below sea level.

Bouvet Island is probably the world's most remote place. No one lives there, and it is 1,050 miles from its nearest neighbor, Queen Maud Land in Antarctica.

A dog named Scooter had to be rescued from an ice floe after chasing a coyote and becoming stranded. The foxhound was carried away to sea in a blizzard and traveled 43 miles over five days.

US explorer Richard Byrd (1888–1957) spent six months of an Antarctic winter living alone in a shack only 9 feet by 13 feet buried beneath the snow.

GOING TO EXTREMES

DRY AS A BONE
DESERTS

Water is a very precious thing in a desert. These arid places get fewer than 10 inches of rain in one year, but in reality many get far less than that. Just one inch of rain falls in Africa's Sahara Desert in an average year!

Imagine a desert and visions of golden dunes, palm-fringed oases, and cloudless skies come to mind. In fact, while some deserts have perfect fields of sand dunes, called ergs, many more are vast, windswept plains covered with stones, gravel, dried-out mud, and salt. About 8 million square miles (or 14 percent) of the Earth's land is desert, and the animals, plants, and people that live here battle for survival in one of Earth's harshest habitats.

The Sahara is the largest desert in the world. It has a total area of about 3.5 million square miles—about as big as the USA. Every year, around 700 people enter the Sand Marathon, which takes place in the Moroccan part of the desert. Competitors race 150 miles across sand dunes, through sandstorms, and in temperatures of 120°F.

Some sand dunes grow to 700 feet high.

The only deserts larger than the Sahara are cold deserts: the Arctic and the Antarctic.

The Sahara crosses 11 countries.

Desert temperatures are hot in the day but fall to below freezing at night.

Ripley's Believe It or Not!®

Hot hideaway

The Sonoran Desert is home to the Couch's spadefoot toad. This clever creature stays underground, only emerging in July when the rainy season comes.

The word "Sahara" comes from the Arabic for "desert."

BLOWN AWAY

As the wind blows across the "Empty Quarter" desert on the Arabian Peninsula, it creates sand dunes. Many dunes are crescent-shaped, but sometimes changes in wind direction form these unusual dot-shapes.

BIG WORD ALERT

WADIS

Dried up riverbeds in the desert. If it rains they fill with water and become rivers again for a short time.

List it!

without eating or drinking.
because it can travel for days in desert conditions
The camel is known as the "ship of the desert"

hottest months.
many accidents and deaths that happen in the
to allow it time to regenerate, and to prevent the
summer! Authorities stop tourists from going there
The Simpson Desert in Australia is closed in

than 20 years.
where no rainfall has been recorded for more
There are parts of the Atacama Desert in Chile

hundreds of ancient Roman cities.
toward the Mediterranean, it swallowed up
southward. As the Sahara Desert grew northward,
present, the Sahara Desert is gradually expanding
Deserts shrink and grow in size over time—at

HOT STUFF

Plane graveyard

The Sonoran Desert in the southwest US is home to a graveyard with a difference: it's where old planes go to die. Rows of them are kept at the Davis-Monthan Air Force Base in Tucson. The dry conditions help to preserve the planes in case they are needed for spare parts, or even to fly again.

Side step

Sidewinder snakes leave distinctive J-shaped tracks in the desert sand. They move sideways and are very fast.

Life support

An oasis is a rare place in a desert where water is close enough to the surface to form springs, streams, and small lakes. However, around three quarters of the oases in the Sahara Desert are man-made. Water is directed to chosen places to allow trees to grow, giving valuable shade from the non-stop sunshine.

PASTURES NEW
GRASSLANDS

Grass is one of nature's top success stories— it's almost indestructible! This hardy plant can survive wildfires, and being grazed, mown, frozen, scorched, trampled, and blasted by high winds.

Grass grows shoots at ground level, so even if its long, narrow leaves are damaged, it can recover. It grows where there is too little rain for trees, and too much rain for deserts to form. In warm temperate zones, grasslands are called prairies, steppes, veldts, and pampas. In the hot tropics, grasslands are called savannas and some types of savanna grasses can grow to 25 feet high.

Zebras eat only the top part of grass stalks, leaving the rest for different types of animals.

No flight zone

Ratites are a family of flightless birds that live in grassland areas of the world. The ostrich lives in Africa, the emu lives in Australia, and the rhea lives in South America. An ostrich eye measures almost 2 inches across and is as big as its brain—about the size of a walnut.

"Are you saying I'm nutty?"

Savanna is grassland with a few trees that provide valuable food and shade for animals.

Mighty mound

he savanna is home to huge ermite mounds and acacia rees. Clay mounds of 10 feet re common, but some giants each 30 feet high. Acacia rees provide food for many animals—even the roots are eaten by porcupines. The trees have sharp thorns to protect them, but a giraffe's tongue is so leathery it can eat the leaves without feeling pain.

HOME ON THE RANGE

In 1800, the prairies of North America were home to herds of wild bison (buffalo) that contained up to 30 million animals. In 2010, the Bridges family house in Texas is home to a single buffalo called Wildthing! He is allowed into their house, except when he is in a bad mood, when his 2,000-pound bulk makes him too dangerous to live in a small space.

twist it!

MUCHAS GRASSES

The elephant grass that grows on the savannas of India can reach 25 feet in height.

A large swarm of locusts can strip an area of grassland the size of Manhattan—in a day, eating about 20,000 tons of vegetation.

The savannas in the cerrado region of Brazil and Paraguay are home to about 5 percent of the world's animal species.

Savannas have long, dry winters with about 4 inches of rain, and shorter summers with up to 25 inches of rain each month.

Natural grasslands cover nearly 4 million square miles of Earth's surface.

>>Hiding space <<

When baobab trees lose their leaves in the dry season they look as if they are stuck upside down in the ground! The massive trunk becomes hollow as the tree gets older. These hollow spaces have been made into homes, chapels, a post office, a pub, and even a toilet!

WILD WOODLANDS

CONIFEROUS AND TEMPERATE FORESTS

Life is harsh near the North Pole, and plants struggle to survive when temperatures drop. Conifer trees, however, can cope with the cold, and grow in enormous forests that stretch around the globe. Also known as needle-leaf trees, conifers cover around 6.4 million square miles through North America, Europe, and Asia.

Moving south, the weather warms up. Here in the wet and mild temperate zone deciduous trees grow and create a habitat for woodland life such as deer and foxes. When winter approaches, the trees lose their leaves, settle down for a long nap, and wait for spring.

The Siberian larch is probably the world's most widespread conifer.

The trees' sap contains "antifreeze" so water inside the tree doesn't freeze.

Coniferous trees have thin needle-shaped leaves that generally remain on the tree throughout the year. They do not have flowers, but produce their seeds inside cones. These open in dry weather so that the seeds can be blown away by the wind, and close in damp conditions to keep the seeds safe.

Nature's giant

The largest single living thing on Earth is a coniferous tree. The Giant Sequoia known as "General Sherman" in California is nearly 275 feet high and weighs an estimated 2,500 tons. Usually, these trees grow to at least 165 feet: the height of 40 ten-year-olds standing on top of each other!

CONIFEROUS

SPRING

SUMMER

FALL

WINTER

Green, Amber, Red

Deciduous trees go through a yearly cycle. In spring and summer, buds unfurl, blossoms bloom, and the tree sports its full crowning glory of leaves. In fall, the trees start to lose their leaves ready to preserve energy in the cold winter months. Many trees are famous for their glorious fall colors of red, orange, and gold.

TREE TIME

Siberia contains 20 percent of the world's forests, and 50 percent of the world's coniferous forests.

Miners in Hungary in 2007 were digging for coal but found instead an eight-million-year-old forest! The 16 trees they discovered were all fossilized but were still wood, instead of turning to stone as trees often do when buried.

A sycamore tree in Scotland has "swallowed" a bicycle that was left against it for years, and grown around the metal with its trunk. The tree has gradually handlebars!

Around 200 petrified trees were discovered by Clyde Friend on his land in Washington State. The forest contained maple, elm, hickory, and sweetgum trees, and was preserved over 15 million years ago when it was covered by lava.

DECIDUOUS

A 200-year-old chestnut tree in Dorset, England, had to be chopped down in 2007 because of wood rot. Amazingly, the tree surgeons found the image of a tree in one of the branches! The shape was caused by the disease in the wood.

The root of the problem

A pine tree stump in Michigan has been left high and dry by erosion. The tree was felled and after 40 years of being blown by the wind, the roots were left exposed 6 feet above the ground.

Tree people

This man is actually a living, growing tree! He was created by Peter and Becky Cook of Queensland, Australia. They carefully grow and graft trees into their chosen design, and have also made a growing chair strong enough for you to sit on.

STEAMY SURROUNDINGS

TROPICAL RAINFORESTS

Trekking through a warm, wet tropical rainforest is tough. Enormous trees, hanging vines, and large, lush leaves fill every available space and it can be a battle to make any headway.

Rainforests contain a bigger range of animals and plants than anywhere else on Earth. Just 1 acre might contain up to 120 different types of tree. Because the rainforest floor is dark, the trees have tall, straight trunks so their upper branches can reach the sunlight, and create a canopy 150 feet high.

GREEN SCENE

The tallest rainforest trees are known as emergents because they emerge above the canopy. In Sarawak, Malaysia, the species *Koompassia excelsa* grows to heights of more than 262 feet.

The rainforest talipot palm blooms with over 20 million individual flowers.

A quarter of the medicines we have today owe their existence to rainforest plants.

The canopy trees are packed so closely together that it can take ten minutes for rain to get through and reach the ground.

twist it!

Several rainforest frogs use their bright colors to warn off hungry predators. Certain species ooze poison through their skin. Many are called "poison dart frogs" as some rainforest tribes were said to smear the poison on the tips of their darts for hunting—although they are far more likely to use poisonous plants for this.

The hot lips plant has special leaves that look— you guessed it—just like bright red lips. It grows in the rainforests of Ecuador in South America.

The Rafflesia plant of the Sumatran rainforest bears a single flower that measures up to 3½ feet in diameter and smells like rotting meat.

THE WANDERER

The wandering spider lives in Brazil, and is responsible for more human deaths than any other spider. This one is eating a termite. Their name comes from their habit of wandering through the forest rather than making webs.

The monkey slug caterpillar has pairs of hairy "legs" that make it look more like a tarantula than a caterpillar. Underneath, it has normal legs, body, and head. The fake legs can sting for added protection.

HAIRY SCARY

Larger than life

Tropical rainforests cover about 4.4 million square miles of the Earth's surface. The largest is the Amazon rainforest with an area of about 2.3 million square miles, across nine countries. More than half the world's rainforests are found in just three countries: Brazil, Democratic Republic of the Congo, and Indonesia.

The longest stick insects in the world live in the rainforests of Borneo and can be 20 inches long. Many rainforest species grow extremely large. The titan beetle of the Amazonian rainforest (see below) is one of the biggest insects in the world, reaching lengths of 6½ inches.

Actual size!

EARTH IN DANGER

TIME IS RUNNING OUT

Twenty thousand years ago the Earth was in the grip of an Ice Age, and massive sheets of ice reached as far south as London and New York. Since then, the world has been slowly but gradually getting warmer.

The Earth's climate has been changing for billions of years; sometimes it's hotter than today, sometimes it's colder. However, scientists believe that the global warming we are experiencing now is not just a natural phenomenon. It's thought we humans are making it worse by putting more carbon dioxide (CO_2) gas in the atmosphere, by burning fossil fuels.

Going under

The city of New Orleans is on the shifting delta of the Mississippi River, and its highest point is only 6 feet above sea level. Its residents have always lived in fear of hurricanes and flooding. Now scientists are warning that rising sea levels will surround the city and cut it off from the mainland, probably within 100 years.

Man-made climate change is having such an effect on the world's plants and animals that a quarter of all species could die out in years, not centuries. Some scientists suggest that Australia could lose more than half of its types of butterfly by 2050.

Hurricane Katrina in 2005 caused over 125 billion dollars-worth of damage and left tens of thousands of people with no home.

Heating up

Global warming has one certain effect: ice begins to melt. At both poles, the ice sheets are getting smaller. Large chunks fall into the sea. Scientists have recorded rising sea levels of about 0.1 in each year, and are worried that they may be 3 feet higher by the end of the century.

>> Chopped down <<

Massive parts of the world's rainforests are being cut down to make room for farms and roads, and to provide timber. An area of rainforest the size of two soccer pitches is destroyed every second. This leaves local people, and some of the world's rarest animal species, with nowhere to live.

>> Bottles banked <<

Not everyone throws away their trash. Maria Ponce of El Salvador has built a whole house out of empty plastic bottles!

SAY WHAT?

Mount Rumpke is the highest point in Hamilton County, Ohio, (1,000 feet) and is completely made of garbage.

Filling up

Our planet is getting full: full of people, homes, farms, cars, cities... we're running out of space. The more people crowd onto our planet, the harder it is for the Earth to supply the food, fuel, and land we need. One billion people (a sixth of the world's population) live in shanty towns, which are made up of thousands of shelters built from scraps, squashed into dangerously small, unhealthy spaces.

Thrown away

More people make more waste. We now know that it's better to reuse whatever we can, instead of filling our trash or making new things. Burying our rubbish underground can be bad for the environment, and producing new cars, TVs, and all the items we use in modern life takes up valuable energy and materials.

#

ACKNOWLEDGMENTS

COVER (sp) © Tanguy de Saint Cyr/Fotolia.com, (c) © Andrew Evans/iStock.com; **2** (b) Action Press/Rex Features, (t) Patrick Landman/ Science Photo Library; **3** Dan Belcher www.ampersandworkshop.com; **4** (b/l) © Andrew Evans/iStock.com; **4–5** (t) ©Suzannmeer.com/ Fotolia.com; **5** (b) Yang Fan/ChinaFotoPress/Photocome/Press Association Images; **6** (b) © Eric Isselée/Fotolia.com, (b/c) AFP/Getty Images, (b/r) © iStock.com; **6–7** (dps) © Srecko Djarmati/Fotolia.com; **7** (t/l, t, t/r, b/l, b, b/r) © iStock.com; **8** (c) © Lorelyn Medina/ Fotolia.com, (b) Mikkel Juul Jensen/Bonnier Publications/Science Photo Library, (b/r) Patrick Koster/Barcroft Media Ltd; **8–9** © Jan Rysavy/iStock.com; **9** (t/r) David Parker/Science Photo Library, (b) Patrick Koster/Barcroft Media Ltd; **10** (sp) Reuters/Masaharu Hatano (t/r) © iStock.com; **11** (t/l) Sipa Press/Rex Features, (b/r) Stringer Shanghai/Reuters, (b/c) Photolibrary.com; **12** (b) © Peter McBride/ Aurora Photos/Corbis; **12–13** (dps) Ethel Davies/Robert Harding/Rex Features, (b) Camera Press; **13** (b, b/r) Sergio Pitamitz/Robert Harding/Rex Features; **14** (b) Alex Sudea/Rex Features; **14–15** (sp) Marco Fulle/GB/Barcroft Media; **15** ((b/c) I.B.L./Rex Features, (b/r) Image Courtesy of the Image Science & Analysis Laboratory, NASA Johnson Space Center, (t/r) Kirk Lee Aeder/Barcroft Media Ltd; **16** (l) © iStock.com; (b) © Shaun Lowe/iStock.com **16–17** (c) © Surpasspro/Fotolia.com; **17** (sp) Dr Juerg Alean/Science Photo Library, (t/r) Yang Fan/ChinaFotoPress/Photocome/Press Association Images; **18** (sp) Javier Trueba/Msf/Science Photo Library; **19** (sp) © Cathy Keifer/Fotolia.com, (c) Brian Brake/Science Photo Library, (t/r) Gary Berdeaux/AP/Press Association Images, (b/r) Sam Tinson/Rex Features; **20** (t) © Usefulebooks4u/Fotolia.com, (c) © Tom Bean/Corbis, (b) Alan Blacklock NIWA; **20–21** (sp) © Bsilvia/Fotolia.com; (t) © Stas Perov/Fotolia.com, (b) © Kimberly Kilborn/Fotolia.com; **21** (b/r) © Eric Nguyen/Corbis; **22** (t) © Dan Lockard/Fotolia.com, (b) Kenneth Libbrecht/Barcroft Media; **22–23** Mike Stanford WSDOT; **23** (t) Action Press/Rex Features (c) Photograph by Ray Asgar www. austinhelijet.com, (b) Eric Gay/AP/Press Association Images; **24** (b) © iStock.com, (t/l) Michael Patrick O'Neill/Science Photo Library, (t/r) Norbert Wu/Minden Pictures/FLPA; **25** (b/l) Barcroft Media via Getty Images, (c, t/r) © NHPA/Photoshot, (b/r) Christopher Griner, Woods Hole Oceanographic Institution; **26–27** (b, dps) © iStock.com; **27** (c) © Doug Perrine/naturepl.com, (t/l) Georgette Douwma/ Science Photo Library, (t/r) © David Fleetham/naturepl.com; **28** (sp) © David Woods/iStock.com, (b) Jim Denevan; **29** (b/l) Dan Belcher www.ampersandworkshop.com, (t/r) Reuters/Anwar Mirza, (r) Reuters/Ho New; **30** (b/l) Getty Images; **30–31** Hans-Peter Merten; **31** (www.amazonswim.com; **32** (l) © iStock.com, (r) Roberto Rinaldi/Bluegreenpictures.com; **33** (l) © Martin Harvey/Corbis, (b/r) Christian Pondella/Barcroft Media Ltd, (t/r) © iStock.com; **34** (sp) Larry Broder, (b/l) Kev Cunnick, (t/r) Ho New/Reuters; **34–35** © iStock.com; **35** (sp) Geoff Renner, (b/l) © iStock.com, (b/c) © Staphy/Fotolia.com, (t/r) George Steinmetz/Science Photo Library; **36** (sp) AFP/Getty Images, (b/r) Rodger Jackman; **37** (t/l) © George Steinmetz/Corbis, (t/r) Getty Images, (c) © NHPA/Photoshot, (b) © BasPhoto/Fotolia. com; **38** (b/l) © Irina Igumnova/iStock.com, (t/r) © Nyiragongo/Fotolia.com; **38–39** © Markus Divis/iStock.com; **39** (t) Sherron Bridge (c) Photolibrary.com, (b) © iStock.com; **40** (sp) © Marco Maccarini/iStock.com, (b/l) © Dmitry Naumov/Fotolia.com, (b/c) © Fantasist/ Fotolia.com, (b/r) © Urosr/Fotolia.com; **41** (sp) © Stephan Levesque/iStock.com, (t/l) © iStock.com, (tr) © Olga Shelego/Fotolia.com, (t/bl) © Rxr3rxr3/Fotolia.com, (t/br) © Sean Gladwell/Fotolia.com, (c) Bournemouth News & Pic Service/Rex Features, (b/r) Pooktre. com; **42** (l) © iStock.com, (b/c) Dr Morley Read/Science Photo Library, (b/r) © Dejan Suc/iStock.com; **42–43** (dps) © iStock.com; **43** (t/l) Dr Morley Read/Science Photo Library, (t/r) © Pete Oxford/naturepl.com, (r) Hunter Stark by Tanja Stark (photographer), (b/r) Patrick Landmann/Science Photo Library; **44** (l) © PSD Photography/Fotolia.com; **44–45** (c) David J. Phillip/AP/Press Association Images; **45** (c) © Alberto L. Pomares G./iStock.com, (r) Phil Noble/PA Archive/Press Association Images, (t/r) AFP/Getty Images

Key: t = top, b = bottom, c = center, l = left, r = right, sp = single page, dp = double page, bgd = background

All other photos are from Ripley Entertainment Inc. All artwork by Rocket Design (East Anglia) Ltd.

Every attempt has been made to acknowledge correctly and contact copyright holders and we apologize in advance for any unintentional errors or omissions, which will be corrected in future editions.